DOG BREEDS

Bulldogs

by Sara Green

Consultant:
Michael Leuthner, D.V.M.
PetCare Clinic, Madison, Wisc.

BLASTOFF!
4
READERS

BELLWETHER MEDIA • MINNEAPOLIS, MN

Note to Librarians, Teachers, and Parents:

Blastoff! Readers are carefully developed by literacy experts and combine standards-based content with developmentally appropriate text.

Level 1 provides the most support through repetition of high-frequency words, light text, predictable sentence patterns, and strong visual support.

Level 2 offers early readers a bit more challenge through varied simple sentences, increased text load, and less repetition of high-frequency words.

Level 3 advances early-fluent readers toward fluency through increased text and concept load, less reliance on visuals, longer sentences, and more literary language.

Level 4 builds reading stamina by providing more text per page, increased use of punctuation, greater variation in sentence patterns, and increasingly challenging vocabulary.

Level 5 encourages children to move from "learning to read" to "reading to learn" by providing even more text, varied writing styles, and less familiar topics.

Whichever book is right for your reader, Blastoff! Readers are the perfect books to build confidence and encourage a love of reading that will last a lifetime!

This edition first published in 2010 by Bellwether Media, Inc.

No part of this publication may be reproduced in whole or in part without written permission of the publisher. For information regarding permission, write to Bellwether Media, Inc., Attention: Permissions Department, 5357 Penn Avenue South, Minneapolis, MN 55419.

Library of Congress Cataloging-in-Publication Data
Green, Sara, 1964–
Bulldogs / by Sara Green.
    p. cm. – (Blastoff! Readers dog breeds)
Includes bibliographical references and index.
 Summary: "Simple text and full-color photography introduce beginning readers to the characteristics of the dog breed Bulldogs. Developed by literacy experts for students in kindergarten through third grade"–Provided by publisher.
 ISBN 978-1-60014-297-0 (hardcover : alk. paper)
 1. Bulldog–Juvenile literature. I. Title.
SF429.B85G86 2010
636.72–dc22
                              2009037207

Printed in the United States of America, North Mankato, MN.
010110   1149

Contents

What Are Bulldogs?

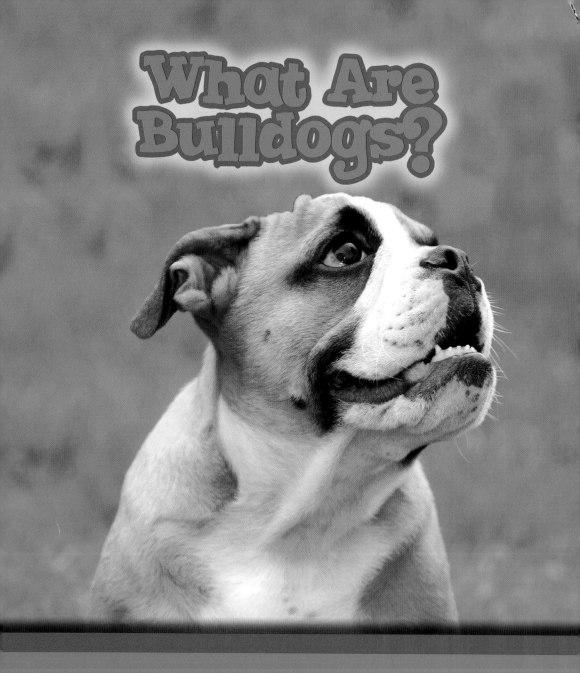

Bulldogs are tough-looking, gentle dogs. They are sturdy dogs with large heads and short legs.

Adult Bulldogs weigh between 50 and 55 pounds (22 and 25 kilograms). They are between 12 and 16 inches (30 and 38 centimeters) tall at the shoulder.

Bulldogs have smooth **coats** that come in many different colors. Common coat colors are **brindle**, red, white, and **piebald**.

Bulldogs have flat faces and short **muzzles**. They have wrinkles in their faces and necks. They have narrow **airways**. The narrow airways cause some Bulldogs to have breathing problems.

Bulldogs have long, hanging upper lips. These are called **chops**. The long chops make Bulldogs look like they are frowning.

chops

Bulldogs have strong jaws. The lower jaw is longer than the upper jaw. This is called an **undershot jaw**.

History of Bulldogs

The **ancestor** of the Bulldog was a large dog called a Molossus. It lived in Asia over 4,000 years ago. Molossus dogs were strong fighters and guard dogs.

People brought the **breed** to England over time. In the 14th century, people began breeding the large dogs to be smaller. These small dogs are thought to be the first Bulldogs.

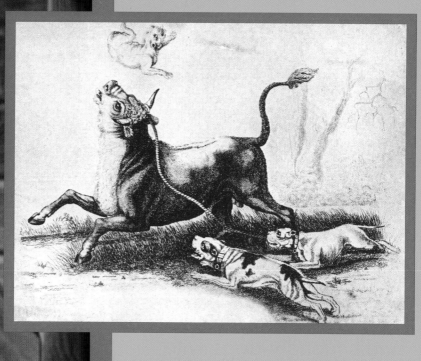

People used Bulldogs to guard bulls. This is how the breed got its name. People noticed that Bulldogs were fearless fighters. They began to use Bulldogs to fight bulls in a sport called bull baiting. Bulldogs were good fighters. Their short, wide bodies could stay low to the ground to avoid a bull's horns.

England outlawed bull baiting in 1835. Some people thought that the Bulldog breed would disappear. Bulldog owners wanted to breed friendly pets. They bred gentle Bulldogs with a breed called the Pug. Pugs are small, friendly dogs with short muzzles. By 1900, Bulldogs had become **companion dogs**.

Pug

Bulldogs Today

The Bulldog is a **non-sporting dog**. These are dogs that once worked or hunted but now live as pets.

Bulldogs do not need a lot of activity. They like to play outdoors, but they get tired easily. Bulldogs are happy to stay inside!

Bulldogs do not bark very much. They make noises in other ways. Bulldogs snore loudly when they sleep. They also snort and wheeze. They make these noises because they have short airways and narrow nostrils.

fun fact

Bulldogs are not good swimmers because they have thick, wide bodies and short legs. Bulldogs should wear life jackets when they are near water.

The look of the Bulldog makes it a popular **mascot** for sports teams. It is also the mascot for the United States Marine Corps.

Bulldogs are strong, loyal, brave, and gentle. It's no wonder so many people make Bulldogs their pets!

Glossary

airway—the path air follows to get into and out of the lungs

ancestor—a family member who lived long ago

breed—a type of dog

brindle—brown with black stripes or spots

chops—the lips of an animal; Bulldogs have long chops.

coat—the hair or fur of an animal

companion dogs—dogs that provide friendship to people

mascot—an animal or person used as a symbol by a group or team

muzzle—the nose, jaws, and mouth of an animal

non-sporting dog—a dog kept mainly as a pet

piebald—spots of different colors on the coat of a dog

undershot jaw—a lower jaw that is longer than the upper jaw

To Learn More

AT THE LIBRARY

American Kennel Club. *The Complete Dog Book for Kids*. New York, N.Y.: Howell Books, 1996.

Meister, Cari. *Bulldogs*. Edina, Minn.: Abdo Publishing, 2002.

Wilcox, Charlotte. *The Bulldog*. Mankato, Minn.: Capstone Press, 1998.

ON THE WEB

Learning more about Bulldogs is as easy as 1, 2, 3.

1. Go to www.factsurfer.com.

2. Enter "Bulldogs" into the search box.

3. Click the "Surf" button and you will see a list of related Web sites.

With factsurfer.com, finding more information is just a click away.

Index